THE STORY OF I

HELEN HAMILTON

BALBOA.PRESS
A DIVISION OF HAY HOUSE

Balboa Press books may be ordered through booksellers or by contacting:

Balboa Press
A Division of Hay House
1663 Liberty Drive
Bloomington, IN 47403
www.balboapress.co.uk
UK TFN: 0800 0148647 (Toll Free inside the UK)
UK Local: 02036 956325 (+44 20 3695 6325 from outside the UK)

Print information available on the last page.

ISBN: 978-1-9822-8375-9 (sc)
ISBN: 978-1-9822-8376-6 (e)

Balboa Press rev. date: 06/28/2021

TABLE OF CONTENTS

Dedicated to all beings.
May we all find peace.

INTRODUCTION

This is really not about me. It is about you and all of us. This book is an autobiography of the Self if such a thing could exist.

Read each chapter and contemplate it before going onto the next. Each chapter is designed to deepen your realisation of the Self and as such the book is written in stages or steps. You may have noticed some of these stages in your own understanding.

In addition to your own self inquiry and practice, this book can provide vital contemplation points to aid in your discovery of what you really are. At times it will seem to contradict itself and not make sense. The true "I" that I speak to in you understands already…I am just reminding you.

At the end of each chapter there are some contemplation points listed. It is advised that you spend some time pondering these points as they are designed to help you to further your understanding and aid in the full realisation of what you are.

There is some space left after each chapter for you to write any notes or insights from your contemplations. There is no final answer to each contemplation but simply just an ever deepening sense of knowing and clarity.

ONE

At first, I was simply the unborn awareness Self. I was everywhere present and yet nowhere in particular. I was all and all was in me. There was no growth, no expansion or transcendence. There was only me.

I could not perceive myself as I was everything and everywhere and there was no reference point to be able to look back at myself from.

I could not experience myself as I was the only thing in existence and there was no time.

I did not know I existed and I did not know anything at all. I could not think. I was all.

Contemplation Points:

1. Why could I not experience myself?

2. Why could I not perceive myself?

TWO

Then a human body appeared in me and inside this body I realised that I exist here. I realised that I am.

With the coming of this body I knew that I was and I could think "I am".

I was existence itself and that was all I knew. I knew I am. I thought to myself "I am here".

There was perception of my existence.

Contemplation Point:

1. Why did the appearance of a human body in me allow me to be aware of my existence?

THREE

Then I saw this human body and I recognised that I am this body. I realised "I am this body" and my attention saw this first thing.

This body was the first object that had appeared and I felt joy in identifying with this new thing in my awareness.

Over time I learned to value other things and to search for them. I began to value other thoughts such as thoughts about myself, my body, my thoughts and much more. I began to define myself and my world only by the things I could see.

My belief that I am this body became very firmly established as I was fascinated learning how to move this body and what it could do. I could use it to experience my world.

A collection of thoughts began to grow inside my head. These were thoughts that I thought so often that I began to call them "my mind" as it felt safe to me.

I began to know myself as the body and all the things that I called "mine" became highly valued such as my family, my mind, my likes and dislikes.

When I learned to value things I soon forgot about my no-thing awareness Self and when this body died one day I seemed to disappear. I forgot about my real Self and that this body appeared in me.

More bodies came and went, and each time I thought that I was this body and that I was coming and going, being born and dying each time.

Contemplation Points:

1. Why did I forget about my no-thing awareness Self?

2. What happened to me after each body died and before another one came?

FOUR

One day, I began to feel fear that I would die. I began to notice my body ageing and beginning to fail. I saw other people ageing and dying and I began to fear the end of my existence. Over time this became stronger and stronger and over many bodies this fear eventually became so strong that I could not even really enjoy this current body.

A new thought came to me one day that said "I wonder if this is all there is to existence?" I began to question life and existence and to ask if there was more to life than I knew.

Over time I became obsessed with this search and began to look everywhere I could for an answer. Reading books, meditating…all the time consumed by this inner drive to find answers, to find an end to this fear. Life could not simply be about being born, experiencing for a few years and then dying and it all being wiped out.

I began to notice that other people did not feel this drive or seem to have so much fear. Or perhaps they were better at ignoring it than me.

I tried very hard to get many things that would distract me from my search and my fear but none of it worked.

Contemplation Point:

1. Did others have the same fear that I did? If so, why did they not show it?

FIVE

One day a new thought came and it said "I must have come from somewhere. Even if I am only this body then the succession of bodies and parents must have started somewhere. I must have an origin that was not a body".

Suddenly this thought made a lot of sense. I realised I could not only be this body. I began to see that I am inside this body and I was wearing this body.

It seemed obvious that I am the "I" inside this body.

I felt a bit happier knowing that I was not only this body although I noticed that I still needed this body to exist. I had no memories of anything before this body and I began to feel the dread again. The ever present threat of non-existence loomed again so my search continued. Still, I felt I was making progress.

I couldn't actually find myself when I looked for me but I knew that I was associated with this body.

Contemplation Points:

1. Why did I have no memories of before this body arrived?

2. What actually is our mind?

SIX

Then I had a thought that perhaps it is the same "I" in all human bodies. It made sense to me. Everyone else around me seemed to be experiencing birth, life and death and during that life they always called themselves "I" just like I did.

It seemed suddenly obvious that this "I" was experiencing life through all the bodies and it was calling itself a human being each time. It was the same "I" having experiences, successes, failures, families, joy, suffering and all of it. It was the same "I" being born, growing into adulthood, having its own children and ageing. It was all the same "I" ultimately that had to disappear back into the oblivion of death.

This made me a little happier because I was in every human as every human. But still each human had to die eventually.

Contemplation Point:

1. Why was my search for myself not ended at this point? Why was there no satisfaction in this realisation?

SEVEN

One day it occurred to me that everything that existed was being born and dying. Even a cloud had a beginning and an ending. It seemed to make sense that everything that ever had an existence was coming and going. Perhaps then existence meant having a start, duration of lifespan and an ending that was death.

I thought about this a lot and it seemed that not only human beings had an "I" in them but so did the animals. Birds, reptiles and even inanimate objects all followed this pattern of existence.

It occurred to me that even the universe itself was following this pattern.

I realised that what I am is all of creation. I am everything that exists and will exist and has existed. What I am is the whole universe.

Suddenly I could see that I was everything that was manifest, I was everything that was a thing!

For a while I felt immense joy and a sense of everlasting existence, for even though this body was bound to die and I would have to stop experiencing through it, I was eternal after all. I was the first beginning and I will exist until the last ending. I am all of time.

Life itself was what I am. I am everywhere that anything exists and I experience life through and as each thing.

Contemplation Points:

1. What does it mean to be manifest? How would we recognise something as having "manifested"?

2. Is there anything other than the manifest existence?

EIGHT

Soon this joy began to fade and the restlessness that I had before returned. My search seemed not to be finished.

Questions began to arise and I asked myself "If I am all that exists and I am constantly coming and going - where then do I originate from?" It seemed clear to me that everything must be coming out of something that was else or other to me. It seemed to me that there must be some source of existence or nothing could arise and have an existence at all.

For a while I was more confused than ever. My search deepened and I saw that this body, this mind and all bodies and minds, all creation came from a source that was not coming and going. I began to notice a silent space of awareness that was simply here. I could not classify it as existing or not existing because it had no ending or beginning.

Perhaps this was the end of my search? Finally I had found something that was permanent and not subject to change. It was unmanifest and pervaded all of existence. It was the awareness Self that is the source of all existence. I was overjoyed with happiness but the question still remained of how this affected me.

I became intensely curious about this awareness Self and over time I began to see that this awareness is what I am. It seemed obvious finally that I was the one looking at all existence! I could not see comings and goings if I was myself coming and going.

Suddenly existence itself seemed like a dream. I could not be that which was coming and going and even if I was, there must be something more permanent that I am also.

Over time I became established in the realisation that I was the unmanifest source of existence and that all existence was coming out of me.

Contemplation Points:

1. Why must the source of all that exists be the Unmanifest?

2. Why was the sense of existence itself suddenly dream-like?

NINE

Soon an itch began to emerge, something irritated me and it seemed my understanding of myself was still not complete somehow. I began to question how there could be anything other than the unmanifest. Surely anything that arises from my unmanifest awareness Self must also be me too?

I pondered this deeply as the manifest and ever changing world of existence seemed to be completely the opposite of me; it was coming and going and I was infinitely always. It was growing and changing and I had never changed. It was happening in time and yet time happened in me.

One day a realisation appeared in me that perhaps the manifest existence of forms was not real. Perhaps it was all only an appearance. Perhaps things being born was simply only a change of appearance from being invisible and unmanifest to being manifest. Perhaps nothing was actually born at all. Maybe nothing died either but simply the appearance of it changed back to its original unmanifest state of being invisible and intangible.

The more I thought about it the more joy I felt. I realised that I am allness. I am inclusive of everything including manifest and unmanifest. I am that place where such division does not abide. I am the place before thoughts in which thoughts appear and seem to divide myself.

Peace at last seemed here. Finally I could rest knowing myself to be the All. I knew myself to be everything, nothing and not limited by those terms and by any definition. I am nowhere, everywhere and beyond. I am inside this body, outside this body, supporting this body and beyond both definitions. I am beyond all limitations.

"I" was simply the awareness Self playing as life, existence and all that is. Yet I remain unchanged by anything.

Contemplation Points:

1. Are there any concepts or definitions that apply to me now?

2. If I cannot be described by thoughts, ideas and concepts then how have I come to recognise myself? Can my mind be recognising this ultimate conclusion or is it something else?

TEN

Then one day I realised that none of this actually happened.

I realised this journey that I had been on was only a story.

I realised "I" am only a dream I am having inside the real me which has always been and will be and I was happy.

I marvelled at what a vivid imagination I have!

Contemplation Points:

1. Is there any such thing as liberation or bondage?

2. Can the sense of "other" or "else" continue here? Is there anything other than me?

NOTES

APPENDIX

The following information is included as an excerpt from Helen's book "Dissolving the Ego" to help you grasp what You really ARE and what You really are not. It can be challenging to learn to perceive That which is not an object and this appendix is intended to help you to do so.

What is the Noumenon?

The Noumenon is what you are, but you have been taught to think of yourSelf as a phenomenon.

The Noumenon is a very useful name for what you really are and as such it will always be capitalised in this book. It is useful to look at the classical definition of the Noumenon, and the "opposite" of it which is a phenomenon (plural is phenomena):

Noumenon:

- A thing as it is in itself, as distinct from a thing that is knowable by the senses.
- A thing which is knowable only without the use of ordinary sense perception.
- A thing that cannot be experienced through the senses.

Phenomenon:

- The object of a person's perception
- A fact or situation that is observed to exist
- An event, fact or happening that can be observed to occur.

We can see from these definitions that the Noumenon is something that you cannot experience through the physical senses; we cannot see it, taste it, touch it or smell it. We can also know that the Noumenon is not something that has a finite existence in time, meaning it has no start or ending. We can contrast this with a phenomenon which has a distinct start and end in time and has a duration or lifespan. A phenomenon can be seen, felt, touched or experienced. The Noumenon cannot.

We cannot come to know what we are and live as That by using just the methods that have worked in the past. We have been taught to gather knowledge and to learn about things and to acquire information. We have also been taught to value above all else the tangible world of objects and events; to judge what we can see, feel, hear, taste, touch or think about as real. We have also been conditioned to totally disregard what is invisible, intangible and formless. A good analogy is the moment we enter a room, we immediately look at the objects in the room but totally ignore the space in it or the air in it. If we see a lake or a body of water we immediately look at the birds floating on the surface and not the water. In this way we immediately bypass the obvious Noumenon that is the Silent Field in which all objects and phenomena appear.

Phenomena come and go. The Noumenon Is, always.

Phenomena of Thought

We have a habitual tendency to define ourselves by what we see; we think we are what we see. The first thing most of us notice is a sense of being someone that is made up of the phenomena of thoughts about ourselves. These can be thoughts about our history, our potential future, or dreams, hopes or goals, our desires and much more. We notice immediately this collection of familiar thoughts and we call it "me" and "my mind". We do not stop to notice that these thoughts appear in something that can recognise thoughts but ITSELF IS NOT A THOUGHT.

Thoughts are the first phenomena to appear in the Noumenon. The Noumenon is Silent, Infinite, Still, Peaceful, Invisible, Intangible and beyond time and space and yet all things appear in It. The first thing to appear in it is the thought "I am" or "I exist". After this, a whole lifetime's worth of thoughts are accumulated and we are systematically trained to pay more attention to what appears *in* the Noumenon than *the* Noumenon Itself.

How many times a day do you stop to look at what is looking at your thoughts?

How many times a day do you listen to your listening?

Have you ever wondered what is watching the endless succession of thoughts come and go?

Have you ever wondered why your attention ALWAYS goes to what you are thinking and NEVER goes to what is noticing the thinking?

Even the sense of "me" is not permanent. It was not here last night in deep sleep but it re-emerges every morning to feature throughout the whole waking day, then disappears again as you go to sleep. Even this sense of "me" is a phenomenon appearing in You — the Noumenon.

It does not matter if these are merely words for you right now. In time you will come to live from this place CONSCIOUSLY (you already are the Noumenon but It has not as yet recognised Itself). Apply what you learn in this book and all that will change.

Learn to discriminate between form and formlessness. Learn to discern what is You and what is not you. Thoughts, emotions, perceptions, opinions, events, relationships, sensations and bodies all have a beginning and an ending and as such have to be phenomena and will not stay. Everything you can perceive is not the True You. Even this sense that "I am conscious/awake/aware" is not the True You. Use the tools in this book to take you to the Highest Place and make a stand there.

Change of Values and Habits

In this process we are really only turning around two habits:

Habit 1 — To value phenomena above that which they arise in. To value phenomena as the most important thing (including thoughts!).

Habit 2 — The habit of putting all of our attention on what comes and goes and giving no attention at all to what is Eternal.

Gradually we will turn around these habits by redirecting our attention back to the Noumenon again and again until this becomes the predominant habit. It is as simple as that. As we focus on what we really are, the delusions about ourselves begin to fall away. It is like pricking a hole in a balloon and watching the air begin to leak out. At some point the balloon is lifeless and empty. We simply need to stop the habit of feeding attention to the phenomenon of the egoic sense of "me". This redirection of attention happens gradually over time for most people, but is accelerated by the practices in this book.

You cannot simply stop a habit but you can replace it with another. We can replace the habit of looking at our thoughts, emotions and body and believing we are them. We can begin to put attention on the Noumenon and gradually it becomes more and more clear that this is what we have always been.

You can succeed at turning around these habits because they were not original to you. It takes effort and energy to keep the attention focused on thoughts and it was not easy for you when you were small to learn to do this. Any habit can be turned around with consistent effort and soon you will revert back to your natural state.

The Noumenon is not some far away mystical concept. It is That which hears the inner speech of thoughts and outer speech of words. It is That which sees the inner images in the mind and outer images of the physical world.

The question "What is the Noumenon?" is heard by the Noumenon! This sense of "me" is not what you think it is!

NOUMENON	PHENOMENON
Oneness	many
Allness	separation
Empty Mind	full mind
Unity	multiplicity
Silent Mind	noisy mind
Non-Duality	duality
"I" as Consciousness	"I" as a person
Nothingness	somethingness
Awakeness	sleep/dream
Consciousness	unconsciousness
Silence	sound
Subjectivity	object
Being	being someone/ something
Stillness	movement
Presence	person
God	ego
Truth	falsehood
Formless	form
Reality	illusion
Knowingness	knowing about
Awareness	perception
Context	content
Infinite Field	finite being
Timeless	duration

If you would like more information about Helen Hamilton, her live Satsangs, silent retreats and classes please contact us:

Our website is www.helenhamilton.org

Find us on Facebook by searching @satsangwithhelenhamilton

Search for us on YouTube at "Satsang With Helen Hamilton"

Email us at evolutionofspirit@gmail.com

Printed and bound by CPI Group (UK) Ltd, Croydon, CR0 4YY